Printed in the United States of America

First Printing, 2015

ISBN-13: 978-1511883597

ISBN-10: 1511883596

Global Computek inc
200 78th Avenue North
St Petersburg FL 33702

www.globalcomputekinc.com

Dedication

I dedicate this book to my Son and daughter Love you guys! You're the center of my life, the force that together with my faith, kept me going.

Table of Contents

Prologue

THERE IS MUCH TALK TODAY about the need to fix the immigration system in the United States. That it is broken and no longer a functioning pathway to immigration and citizenship, I believe is obvious to all.

While most of the discussions have centered around illegal aliens already in the US and creating a mechanism for them to come in from out of the shadows, the problems in the immigration system go much deeper than just illegal aliens. There are multitudes of problems that can lead to deportation even for those who legally go through the system. The process in its current form dehumanizes immigrants, tramples upon their rights and tears them away from family and loved ones and costs enormous amounts of money while accomplishing neither its stated goals as an Agency nor a viable means for expeditious and legitimate entry into the United States.

I know. It happened to me.

I had arrived in the US from Lagos, Nigeria, seeking political asylum from the political oppression in my country. I did not hide nor "slip into" the country through its porous borders. I declared my intention to seek political asylum upon my arrival at JFK Airport in New York City. During my time here since arriving, I married a US permanent resident (who later became a US citizen). We had two children. I was legally working, paying taxes and contributing to society via my work, my church and my family. Never was I using resources of welfare or social services.

I had been in the US for ten years when, without cause or reason, I was arrested and ultimately deported.

This after having tried to immigrate legally and according to the tortuous and labyrinthine process established by the Immigration Service, known today as Immigration and Customs Enforcement (ICE),a division of Homeland Security, which would ultimately only let me down and cost me everything that was dear to me- my family.

In addition, I was physically beaten. Nearly choked to death. Cheated by lawyers who took my money and then never even bothered to even show up in court. Moved from jail to jail across state lines by the Immigration Service to remove me from the jurisdiction where my action was to be heard. All in an effort to wear me down.

Most immigrants caught up in the system do not fight because the system is not set up for justice. It is set up to get as many immigrants deported out of the country as possible.

Which is why I want to tell my story through this book. It needs to be heard and to offer words of encouragement and support to those facing a similar situation.

Today, there is much in the news about the need for immigration reform. Indeed it must be reformed because the process is genuinely broken. I, and many others of my acquaintance, tried to do the right thing and not slink into the United States and remain as illegals.

We however were punished while under the proposed immigration law changes, illegals are being rewarded.

Though there is something inherently unjust about that, it is not the main issue. Don't get me wrong, there is certainly need for reform to address the issues of illegals in this country.

But the main issue is that the system as it exists now strips the dignity from a man. It opens the door toward institutional abuse, such as when the Immigration Service moved me from district to district to thwart my legal efforts to have my case heard and adjudicated. But most importantly, the system as it is now, needlessly destroys families.

I was not a terrorist. I was not a criminal, neither in the US nor in Nigeria. I was not a parasite, leaching money and benefits from social services. I am an educated man and a Christian, then and now. Did I not deserve even a modicum of human dignity, to not be treated like a dog, beaten, choked, lied to and deceived? Don't *all of us* deserve that same human dignity?

Read my story and decide for yourself whether or not the system of immigration in the United States needs to be changed.

Historically, throughout its history, it's been immigration that has given the United States its strength, resiliency and innovation, in all areas, not just industry. Let's not destroy the strength upon which this country was built but renew it in a way that we can once again draw from our immigrant populations the raw strength, energy and talent that has made this country great.

Chapter 1

IT WAS ABOUT 5:00 O'CLOCK in the morning at the New Orleans Parish Prison in New Orleans, Louisiana when the guard came and woke me up. "You're going home," he said. I leaped off the cot. I had just recently filed a Writ of Habeas Corpus with the United State District Court for the Middle District of Georgia asking Judge G. Mallon Faircloth to release me from the Immigration Service's custody as the Service had illegally detained me. I was, after all, legally in the United States. Judge Faircloth must have agreed with me and ordered my release!

I gathered my few things and waited for the officers to release me from the jail. They came to get me and I was driven to the Immigration Service office in downtown Atlanta, GA. Since this was where I had been taken into custody, I just assumed this was part of the release procedure.

I spent the better part of the day in the basement holding facility of the Atlanta Immigration Service offices. There was no paperwork to fill out. I was starting to get a little concerned but convinced myself that it was still just part of the process.

Towards the end of the day, plainclothes officers came and said "Let's go". Finally! I could almost *taste* my freedom. We all got into a car and drove away. I asked if it wouldn't be easier if I just took a bus to my home. The officer just laughed.

My concerns began to increase. Then I saw road signs for the Hartsfield–Jackson Atlanta International Airport. I knew what going to the airport meant. Deportation! I began to panic but the officers said nothing.

We arrived at the airport. I began explaining that I had an open case, that no decision had been made, that I had filed a writ of habeas corpus and couldn't be deported without my case being adjudicated by a judge, that the Immigration Service could not make that decision arbitrarily. I asked if a decision had been rendered and if so that I be provided a copy of the judge's decision and order. After all, a motion for a 20 days extension of time to file an answer to the writ (or otherwise plead) was filed by State Attorney James Letten only a few days prior. Even if the decision had gone against me, I knew enough that I had the right to appeal and could not, legally, be summarily deported.

I was still laying out my arguments when we entered the airport. Finally, the officer turned to me and said that they were doing me a favor. That this wasn't a standard deportation trip, that I would be flying KLM, a commercial airline. That there was a stopover in Amsterdam, the Netherlands, where I could get off and claim political asylum as such asylum had just been granted to eight individuals from Somalia.

I told them I was not interested in the Netherlands, that my wife and children were Americans and I wouldn't go anywhere without them and repeated that I had a case open in the court. I wanted a disposition of that case before I would consider any other option.

They said that it was just too bad, that this was the way it was going to be and that I should be grateful they were doing me this favor instead of sending me to Nigeria on a standard deportation flight. They began to hustle me up the ramp but I started arguing with them again, raising my voice. I yelled that I was in America legally, that I had an open immigration case, that what they were doing was illegal and morally wrong.

People began looking and staring at us. It was obvious the other passengers were becoming concerned, not understanding what was going on and wondering if they were in some kind of danger. Obviously, the Immigration Officers could not do anything physical to shut me up, not in front of all those people.

The flight attendants called out the captain of the plane. He came and the officers tried to explain the situation to him. But I kept interrupting, explaining that what they were saying wasn't true, that I was in the United States legally, that in fact I was being forced on the plane illegally and against my will. That I had an open case before the Court to prove my case and that a decision hadn't been made, that I didn't want to go to Amsterdam because I had a family here that were American citizens, that I had no criminal record nor had I been arrested for any crime, either state or federal, in the US or anywhere else.

I, of course, knew why the Service wanted me out of the country. They were afraid that with the open case, the actions of officers in the Immigration Service would come to light. How I was beaten, choked almost to death, shuttled from state to state so I couldn't press forward with my case, and so much more. But I'm getting ahead of myself.

The captain considered the situation and then refused to take me aboard. He noted that I was obviously emotionally upset and angry about the situation. He added that as this was a commercial flight and that he had to put his passengers and their safety above all else. Therefore, in his judgment, it would not be prudent nor in the passengers' best interests to allow me to fly on this flight and he was refusing to allow my boarding the aircraft.

The officers tried to convince him, even tried to coerce him, to allow me to board. But the captain knew his rights and duties and steadfastly refused.

His actions angered the immigration officers but they knew their hands were tied and so left with me still in their charge.

We went to the Atlanta County Jail until they could figure out what to do with me. They had little option but to return me to the Immigration Service's detention jails.

Immediately upon my return to the Etowah County Jail in Gadsden, Alabama, I filed a Notice of Objection to the later claimed "mistaken" attempt at my deportation, done without regard for my Writ of Habeas Corpus, noting that the Service's attempt to "spirit me away" was a only a way to cover up their illegal detention of me. I knew that if I could just get before a judge to explain my case, for which I had full documentation, that I would win upon the merits of my argument.

Back in a cell, lying on a cot, I started to relax from the day's agitations. I knew that I had effectively "dodged a bullet" as it were, and I continued to reflect upon my situation.

Ten years I had been living in the United States. Ten years trying to do the right thing, work through the immigration system to legally remain here. But I was being thwarted by the very system created to allow for the immigration of foreign nationals.

In the process, I was physically beaten. Nearly choked to death, Cheated by lawyers who took my money and then never even bothered to even show up in court. Moved from jail to jail by the Immigration and Naturalization Service (INS) so that when my case came up the judge was forced to say that he couldn't hear it because it was not in his jurisdiction, forcing me to re-file, only to be moved again. All in an effort to wear me down and make me give up. Just like today's "mistaken" deportation attempt.

But they were wrong. I would NEVER give up. For me, it was a fight for survival. And I had right on my side. The Lord would Bless those *"who hunger and thirst for righteousness, for they shall be satisfied."* After all, didn't He say so? I had faith and the conviction of my faith that, in the end, I would prevail.

But I had not taken into account the cost, the "collateral damage" that this fight would cause, that being my loved ones, my family.

In large measure, this is my attempt to explain to my children as well as the rest of the world the pain and the ultimate toll this fight took upon me. But that I had never given up and that I loved my family throughout all of it, that my son and daughter still mean everything to me. That my children, together with my faith, were the source of the strength that sustained me through the years of this fight.

Chapter 2

MY NAME IS FEMI MICHAEL AJAYI, i was born in Lagos, the Lagos, the most populous city in Nigeria and the second fastest-growing city in Africa, in 1967. My father was a businessman, in the import/export trade. My mother took care of the family. That was a job in itself as there were six of us. I had two brothers and three sisters!

We lived a relatively comfortable middle-class life.

But Nigeria was always a tumultuous country, never more evident than in Lagos. Things were bad. Corruption and nepotism in the government of the time were rife. As a young man and an idealist, I believed things could be made better, Much better, As a youth, I became involved in politics to try and bring about change. Peaceful change, through the electoral process.

My involvement in politics culminated in the June 12, 1993 Presidential elections, the first since the military coup 10 years earlier. The very popular businessman Chief Moshood Kashimawo Olawale Abiola, better known as MKO, of the Social Democratic Party, a progressive party, won against Alhaji Bashir Tofa of the National Republican Convention party in what has been called the freest and fairest election in Nigeria's history.

From 1972 until his death Moshood Abiola had been conferred with 197 traditional titles by 68 different communities in Nigeria, in response to the fact that his financial assistance resulted in the construction of 63 secondary schools, 121 mosques and churches, 41 libraries, 21 water projects in 24 states of Nigeria, and was grand patron to 149 societies or associations in Nigeria.

The U.S. Congressional Black Caucus of the United States issued the following tribute to MKO Abiola:

"Because of this man, there is both cause for hope and certainty that the agony and protests of those who suffer injustice shall give way to peace and human dignity. The children of the world shall know the great work of this extraordinary leader and his fervent mission to right wrong, to do justice, and to serve mankind. The enemies which imperil the future of generations to come: poverty, ignorance, disease, hunger, and racism have each seen effects of the valiant work of Chief Abiola. Through him and others like him, never again will freedom rest in the domain of the few. We, the members of the Congressional Black Caucus salute him this day as a hero in the global pursuit to preserve the history and the legacy of the African diaspora."

This singular election overcame barriers of religion and tribal ethnicity for the greater good of Nigeria. Other such "firsts" included:

The most peaceful election ever held since Nigerian independence

The freest and fairest election in Nigeria since its independence

It was celebrated and extolled by local, national and international observers

There was no record of violence, intimidation, removing or "stuffing" of ballot boxes, rigging, multiple voting, etc.

Both the president-elect and his Deputy were Muslim

It was apparent to me that this was a man whom I could wholeheartedly support. And I did.

However, this historic election was annulled by then military ruler Ibrahim Babangida, leading to a crisis that ended with Sani Abacha heading yet another coup later in the year.

The annulment of the elections enraged Nigerians. Street protests became a daily occurrence. Scores of Nigerians were killed as the military cracked down on protesters. A number of us went into exile while many more were jailed for daring to stand up to the military. They literally shut down the nation with daily street protests and prolonged strikes by workers in critical sectors of the economy.

When Abiola stepped forward to claim his mandate, he was arrested and imprisoned. He subsequently died, on June 24, while under house arrest, after drinking a cup of tea in the presence of American diplomats led by Thomas Pickering. The deaths of several prominent Nigerians who were his supporters followed.

The anniversary of this historic election is celebrated even today, more than 20 years later.

But these were the events that set the stage for my needing to flee the country or suffer the same fate as Abiola and the many others who supported him.

Any attempt to change a current power structure can backfire. It's what happened to me. The political candidate I supported was arrested, a victim of the country's political oppression. To save my life, I had to flee. So I did.

Chapter 3

To get out of Nigeria, my contacts had provided me with a passport. Had I not used this passport, I would never have been allowed out of the country and would have been arrested and now sitting in jail as a political prisoner. Or worse.

I had gotten the passport, bought the ticket, packed, said goodbye and left the country all in one day for fear that travel restrictions would have blocked my departure and forced me to remain. Because everything happened so quickly I didn't have much time to reflect on events.

My first real opportunity to catch up to myself was on the plane. It had been hard to say goodbye to family and friends. I was also sad to be leaving Nigeria. The country had such potential, something Abiola had understood.

And, of course, I had no idea what awaited me in this new country of America, or even if I'd be allowed in. Entry refusal and being put back onto a return flight was a real possibility, one that filled me with dread. I knew what would be waiting for me if I had to return.

From Lagos I flew into JFK Airport. New York City. America! I had made it. The enemies in my country were unsuccessful. I was safe now. I had to believe that. Certainly the United States would recognize the seriousness of my position, the danger I was in, and grant me political asylum!

I just followed the crowd after exiting the plane to Customs and Immigration. It was a long line and I was very much afraid about what would happen. I just didn't know what to expect. My self-confidence waivered but I continued on.

When the long line finally wound down to me, I came before the Immigration Officer and declared my request for political asylum. I knew I was in the right. My life was in danger in Nigeria for nothing more than standing up for change, working within the political process. I had discovered a new source of inner strength and conviction. It must have shown through!

The immigration officer called his supervisor, a big man in Uniform. He escorted me to a small office and began questioning me. I explained my situation completely. He asked many questions about the political situation in Nigeria and my involvement in the political process there. I answered him fully and truthfully. With one exception.

Early on, he stated that there were many requests for political asylum, most of which were turned down and the asylum seeker returned to Nigeria. That I should prepare myself for the same result. So, when he asked me my name, knowing that there was a real possibility of my being returned to Nigeria, I told him my surname was "Winter", having just seen an advertisement for winter vacations. After all, if I were sent back, why should I make it easier for the authorities in Nigeria to discover who I really was?

I remember the immigration supervisor laughing. He knew what I had done and why. We continued chatting for some time. Then he gave me paperwork, told me to fill it out and deliver it the US Immigration Offices at Federal Plaza, in Manhattan, recommended I get an attorney and let me go on my way!

I was stunned and absolutely euphoric! I couldn't believe my good fortune.

Chapter 4

I CLASPED THE SHEAF OF PAPERS and my little bit of luggage and jumped into the nearest cab. I wanted to get the hell out of there in case the supervisor changed his mind!

I had some friends as well as contacts that were provided me when I left Lagos. I asked the cab drop me off in Queens and telephoned one of my friends. His name was Kay and was good enough to pick me up. He took me to his apartment where I stayed for about a year or so, sleeping on his couch.

The documents I had been given upon my arrival at JFK required me to appear at the Immigration Offices within two month. After I had rested some and gotten over my jetlag, I started searching for a lawyer. I had every intention of not "disappearing through the cracks" and living in the US illegally. I intended to pursue my asylum request and remain legally, with all attendant rights and privileges of one who is legally in this country.

I found an attorney named Baljiy Singh, Esq. who specialized in immigration matters. I paid him a retainer to represent me at the hearing. This was almost all the money I had in the world. The first hearing was scheduled for October, 1993, but Attorney Singh said he would be away on vacation on that date.

He wrote a note for me to take to the Court requesting the hearing be re-scheduled. I brought the note to Court on the day of the hearing and gave it to the Court Clerk, who passed it on to the

Judge. The Judge re-scheduled the hearing for December, 1993. But my attorney again failed to appear, and so the hearing was re-scheduled yet again. This went on a total of *five* times.

A final hearing had been scheduled for May, 1994. I had tried contacting Attorney Singh many, many times, but to no avail. I was afraid to appear in court with my attorney failing to show up yet again, fearing that it would lead to my immediate arrest and deportation back to Nigeria. So I failed to appear. Not a day goes by that I do not regret that decision. I realize that I made a very bad mistake by not attending that final hearing.

I had been rooming with Kay for about a year now, still sleeping on his couch. Because I didn't have a work visa I was unable to get formal employment. I took odd jobs to make ends meet. I had the opportunity to make significant sums of money if I opted to go the illegal route of course, but that's not the direction I wanted for my life.

Still in all, I was able to save enough money in two years to rent a very small apartment. I was introduced to Heather, the woman who was to become my wife, through a mutual friend. I still remember our first date, dinner at a local restaurant.

We continued dating and our relationship blossomed. I met Heather's family. They approved of me and so we married. Our son Michael was born and then our daughter Rachel. I couldn't have been happier! But the fact that I was still not officially recognized as having been granted asylum continued to weigh heavily upon me.

He said they couldn't find any record of my immigration application or other documentation. I told him I had physical copies of the application and all supporting documentation. That I had retained a lawyer to prepare and file them, which the attorney did. Next thing I knew he had slammed me against the stairwell wall, asked if I had any weapons and began doing a body search. I was never told I was under arrest or anything of the sort.

I had been in the US for the past ten years, in and out of Immigration Service Offices in New York City, all without incident. If they wanted to arrest me, they could have done so at any time during all those years.

He proceeded to push me ahead of him into an office and handcuffed me to a chair. I had hard copies of some of my documents but he refused to recognize them as genuine. He began questioning me in earnest now, asking if I had a criminal record or had been arrested. I told them I had never been arrested or convicted of any crime, neither here in the Unites States nor anywhere else in the world. They took my fingerprints and ran them but found no record of any crime, only confirming what I had already told them.

Another officer came in saying that it looked like I was legitimate and my case in process. But even then the first officer continued to ask me about any criminal past. Again I denied ever having committed any crime. I could see his anger level rising as he could find nothing wrong or illegal.

He grabbed me and put me into a choke hold. I passed out from it. It scared them.

I remember later reading about Eric Garner who was killed by police using a choke hold in July of 2014. The victim kept saying "I can't breathe, I can't breathe". I know *exactly* how he felt. That could just as easily have been me that died.

Yet another example how the system promotes officers who are out of control and show no sense In understanding limits or of right or wrong action.

The unit supervisor, an Officer Prince by name, was called in and removed the immigration officer who had applied the choke hold on me. He examined the bruising on my neck and photographed them. He then left to question the officer who had assaulted me. I could hear them arguing about whether or not I was legitimate and what had happened to necessitate a choke hold.

This Supervisor, Officer Prince, went to meet with the head of the facility to discuss the incident. He returned afterward and asked if I wanted to press charges against the officer who had assaulted me. I told them all I wanted was to get out of there and go home.

He said they still had some questions. I asked if I could call my wife and she could bring further documents proving my claim to be being in the US legally and supporting that my application for permanent residency was in process. He agreed and I made the call.

It was illogical on the face of it, their arresting me. They knew where I was for all those years when we lived in New York City. And besides, if I were illegal, I would do my best NOT to come in contact with Immigration Service officers, never mind walking in the front door to give them my new address!

My wife Heather arrived some short time later with my together with my son and infant daughter. Everyone was in tears. My wife didn't understand what was happening and my children were just afraid. We were a very close-knit family. Heather brought the documents and the filing receipt to prove to the officers and supervisor that my case was legitimate.

In the end though, it didn't matter. They took me to the basement and put me in a cell.

I knew that a cover-up had begun and they needed to get rid of me to avoid my making problems for them as a result of their actions, like choking me nearly to death.

I spent the next three nights in Paulding County Jail. The Jail is located at 25 Industrial Way North in Dallas, GA, about an hour northwest of Atlanta and has a housing capacity of 300. According to their website, the Center claims to "house individuals detained for numerous other jurisdictions including municipal, state, federal and other local agencies".

It further states "the Paulding County Jail operates on the premise that all inmates in our custody are human beings, and while incarcerated are entitled to humane, fair and impartial treatment".

That was not MY experience. When I arrived there I was told to strip down in a shower room and officers proceeded to hose me down like an animal. I could just as easily have showered on my own if I were afforded the opportunity. I remember reading about gulags and camps where people were treated in the same way. The officers didn't think of us as human beings. More like caged animals. They did whatever they could to strip us of any human dignity.

After a short time, I befriended a number of immigrant detainees at the jail including one detainee who had slipped across the border, been caught and deported, but slipped across again. He was awaiting deportation for a second time but confided to me that he was planning on returning yet a third time.

I considered my situation in light of that conversation. If I were deported back to Nigeria, there would be no "slipping across the border". Therefore, I needed to fight. After all, I had right on my side, though at the time, I didn't realize how little that counted for in the legal system!

I was allowed to use the telephone and first called my New York lawyer Moses Apsan to advise him of the situation and ask if he could render me any assistance. I then called my wife to quiet her fears and tell her I was alright. I told her to find a lawyer locally, as attorney Apson advised he was not licensed to practice in Georgia, and to retain him.

She found an attorney named Benjamin Guile. He wanted $4,000 to represent me. I had my wife pay him a retainer of $1,500.

Attorney Guile came to visit me at the Jail and I explained the entire situation to him, including how I was choked and beaten. He wanted to call a press conference immediately. Having a cooler head, I advocated he get me out of the jail first and then we could explore options like press conferences.

I had hired Attorney Guile to investigate my circumstances, bring forward and argue my case to the Immigration Service, including that I had both filed a Change of Status followed by an immigration application as the Spouse of US Permanent Resident, which was reviewed by the Service AND APPROVED by them. That would have settled the question of my legality as an immigrant in this country and gotten me out of detention. After collecting his fee, Attorney Guiles instead moved to reopen my asylum request case, without either my knowledge or consent. He never even bothered to get an affidavit from me in support of his motion, which would have at least made me aware of the action he was taking.

From the beginning, I did not have a feeling of confidence in attorney Guiles, which proved to be prophetic. I had asked him to confer with my original attorney in New York City, Attorney Moses Apsan, to get the facts of my immigration application and its approval. But Attorney Guiles never did and I never saw him again.

In the end, he wrote two motions for the money I paid him, a motion to re-open my original asylum case and later to have me released on bond.

After filing the motion to re-open my original asylum case, Attorney Guile was taken to task and admonished by Judge Gabriel Videla, who, in her judgment denying the motion declared

"The motion to reopen is defective as it lacks (an) affidavit from the respondent setting forth the factual basis for the motion. Statement of counsel unsupported by respondent's affidavit cannot be considered as evidence and cannot be accorded any evidentiary weight.

Respondent's current counsel is hereby admonished for not having adequately reviewed the Record of the Proceeding prior to filling of the motion to reopen and presenting the motion containing misrepresentation regarding the procedural history of this case".

The motion for bond was also subsequently denied. Being released on an immigration bond would have been an excellent option for me.

A bond is money that you pay to the government allowing you to be released from custody and return to your home in the US while you go through proceedings before an immigration judge.

Some detainees do not qualify for bond and there's a list of grounds for automatically not granting bond. They include

a crime involving "moral turpitude"

multiple convictions where the aggregate sentence is five years or more of imprisonment a controlled substance offense or conviction (really, any drug offense, especially drug trafficking)

a prostitution-related offense

terrorist activity

human trafficking

money laundering

an aggravated felony

a firearms offense

drug abuse or addiction

espionage, sabotage or treason

DUI (Driving Under the Influence of alcohol or drugs)

But I had never been arrested for any crime, never mind being convicted of one, nor was I a drug user or trafficker, a terrorist or a member of any other category that would have prohibited me from obtaining an immigration bond.

Yet denied I was and to this day I do not know why. At least with a bond, I would have been able to be with my family while I worked to clear up the issues with the Immigration Service.

Later I found out that I could have asked an Immigration Judge for what's called a "Joseph Hearing" where the Judge decides whether or not you are subject to mandatory detention, and, if not, to be considered for bond. The judge takes into account factors like potential danger to the community, family ties, employment history and ties to the community, all of which I could have shown and would have supported the bail application.

This is something that Attorney Guiles should have pursued or at least advised me about, but he failed me in even this basic counsel.

Essentially, the only positive outcome of his action was that the motion to re-open my asylum case failed, which was actually a good thing insofar as I had filed a change of status and the opening the original asylum case would serve no purpose. What was needed was a decision on my case based on that change of status and subsequent filing and approval of the Spouse of US Permanent Resident Immigration, not a re-opening of the previous asylum application.

After the Judge's decision, Attorney Guile "resigned" from my case. No big surprise there.

Ultimately, I filed a complaint against him with the Georgia State Bar with regard to his handling of my case. I discovered later I was not the first to make a complaint for such negligence. The internet is full of grievances against him.

On the fourth day, I was transferred to Harris County Jail, located at 9825 Highway 116, Hamilton, Georgia. It's southwest of Atlanta, about an hour and a half by car.

According to the Atlanta Business Chronicle in a May 8, 2006 article, the

"detention of (alleged) illegal immigrants is big business for some Georgia jails."

"In Georgia, federal immigration officials don't have their own detention facility, so they rely on local law enforcement authorities to incarcerate illegal immigrants awaiting court dates or deportation. With the passage of tough new state legislation on illegal immigration, some jail officials expect to see more beds filling up with immigration detainees."

Under a contract with the federal government, Colquitt County Jail provides at least 35 of its 260 beds to house immigration detainees, who are grouped together in cells separated from the regular inmates.

Only two other facilities in Georgia have such contracts -- the Atlanta City Jail and the Harris County Jail. Every year they earn hundreds of thousands of dollars by housing thousands of illegal immigrants, who are detained by immigration officials or arrested for committing crimes while living here illegally."

Many believe that housing allegedly illegal aliens is just big business as County Jails make millions of dollars in contracts with Immigration and Customs Enforcement (ICE). Locking up immigrants for a profit!

"The facilities play a critical role in housing detainees who are in limbo between their homelands and the United States -- sometimes waiting for months to be deported. The situation is a bureaucratic balancing act for immigration officials who are charged with investigating, detaining and deporting illegal immigrants."

I know all of these detention facilities in Georgia as I spent time in all of them! As for the detainees "being in limbo" I can attest to the fact that they are often so because of the ineptitude of the Immigration Service in investigating alleged illegal immigration and determining the case a onits merits, and so it employs whatever tactics it can to push through deportation as the "best solution".

My time at Harris County Jail was emotionally very tumultuous for me. My wife came to visit me but didn't bring our children as we didn't want them to see their father behind bars. We were a very close-knit family and it was very emotional for us both. And I missed my children terribly.

But as a Christian, my faith in God and Jesus Christ helped to sustain me. I prayed often and fasted. Still, I was assailed by doubts. Why was I being punished? Had I committed some sin that I was going through this pain and torture? The Devil seeks whatever foothold he can find.

Later I understood that I was to go through this ordeal so that I could understand and appreciate what freedom and liberty meant. So that I could write a book such as this one to expose the decrepit immigration system for what it is and bring into the light the many abuses it perpetrates on immigrants and immigrant detainees based upon my own personal experience.

As I now needed new representation, I hired Attorney Barbara Mobley, who I later learned became a judge in 2005.

To the best of my knowledge, though paid, she did absolutely nothing for my case. I had also asked her to contact my original New York City attorney Moses Apsan, which she too failed to do.

She never interviewed me and except for talking with her by telephone, I never actually even met her. Attorney Mobley, perhaps pacified by the Immigration Service (actually desperate to get me out of the country), filed an appeal to Judge Videla's decision to Attorney Guile's Motion to re-open my asylum case, completely without my knowledge or agreement.

This was not the best legal strategy and I knew it but was unaware she had proceeded on her own initiative to attempt to re-open the original case. To overcome the deficiency in the original filing by Attorney Guiles, she even went so far as to include an Affidavit together with a General Power of Attorney, again, without either my knowledge or consent, and forging my signature to the affidavit! She then proceeded to falsely notarize that forged signature as if I had indeed actually signed it in her presence.

I AT EVERY TIME WHEN HIRING SOMEONE TO BE MY LAWYER, HOPE THAT THEY COULD HELP MY CASE WITH THE COURT. I EXPECTED THAT THE LAWYER SINGH WOULD COME TO THE COURT WITH ME AFTER HIS HOLIDAYS, BUT HE DID NOT. I AM NOT OF A LAW MIND AND COULD NOT BE SURE OF MY HELP FOR MYSELF BY MYSELF. I NEEDED A LAWYER TO EXPLAIN THE FACTS FOR ME IN A WAY SO THE COURTS WOULD UNDERSTAND AND NOT SEND ME BACK TO NIGERIA TO LIVE IN FEAR.

I HAVE GIVEN MY WIFE A FULL POWER OF ATTORNEY TO HANDLE ALL BUSINESS AND LAW MATTERS IN MY BEHALF AS I AM BEING MOVED AROUND GEORGIA TO DIFFERENT JAILS.

Sworn & subscribed before me
This _13th_ day of _February_ 2003.

NOTARY PUBLIC   AFFIANT

This General Power of Attorney shall remain in effect for a period until my release from INS detention, from this date hereof.

If this General Power of Attorney is terminated by operation of law, any person acting in reliance upon it without notice of such termination shall be held harmless.

IN WITNESS WHEREOF, this General Power of Attorney has been executed by OLEFEMI OLUMIDE WINTER aka FEMI AJAYI on February 13, 2003 at Hamilton, Georgia.

OLEFEMI O. WINTER
aka FEMI AJAYI

Sworn & subscribed before me
This _13_ day of February, 2003.

Notary Public

EXHIBIT

37

Interestingly, the internet is rife with complaints about Attorney/ Judge Mobley as well. In fact, in 2010, the Georgia Judicial Commission embarked on an investigation of Judge Mobley, which led to her resignation on Feb 1, 2010. Among others, the charges against her that led to her resignation included making false statements and failing to rule on cases for nearly four years!

I spent about a month or so in Harris County Jail when I was transferred to Colquitt County Jail in Moultrie, GA.

This facility was almost four hours from Atlanta. It was a struggle for my wife to visit me and so, out of necessity, she came only once.

One evening shortly after I arrived there, I saw three State prisoners jumping the barbed wire fence and escaping. Two carefully climbed the barbed wire fence. It took them more than 20 minutes, knowing they could be seen and seized at any moment. The third man was playing lookout, then threw a white shirt over the barbed wire and climbed over in about ten minutes. I doubted that any of the three had help on the other side or any resources to assist them, yet they were willing to take the risk of putting their fate into their own hands in the fight for their freedom.

While I chose not to follow their path and look to escape, their action made a big impression on me and I resolved that I too would take my fate into my own hands in the fight for my freedom.

I resolved to become my own lawyer as I wasn't getting the representation I was expecting from my previous attorneys, with the exception of Attorney Moses Apsan. I didn't quite know how but I knew that was what I must do.

But then I discovered the law library at the Colquitt County Jail and had spent a number of hours perusing immigration law and relevant cases. And then I knew. I would learn everything I could about immigration law and become my own lawyer. That would be how I would "break out" from this prison facility in which I was being illegally held. From that moment, I spent virtually every waking moment of my allowed free time in that law library.

Of course, my choice begs the question why I had to become a "jailhouse lawyer" to learn what rights and options I had available to me in the first place?

But it seemed to me the good Lord agreed with my decision. Through my law reading I discovered the doctrine of Writ of Habeas Corpus.

The Writ of Habeas Corpus literally means "produce the body". Also known as "the Great Writ," habeas corpus gives citizens the power to get help from courts to keep in check government and other institutions that may illegally imprison people. In many countries, for example, police and military personnel, may take people and lock them up for months or even years without due course or charging them at all. Such imprisoned persons have no avenue, no legal channel, by which to protest or challenge their imprisonment.

But the writ of habeas corpus gives jailed suspects the right to ask an appellate judge to set them free there by ensuring people will not be held for long times in prison in violation of their rights.

The petition is filed to show that the court ordering the detention or imprisonment made a legal or factual error. The Writ of Habeas Corpus is the constitutionally bestowed right of a person to present evidence before a court that he or she has been wrongly imprisoned.

The origins of the Writ of Habeas Corpus can be traced to the fourteenth century and became an established part of English common law by no later than 1600. The Writ was therefore part of the law of England and transported by the settlers into the thirteen colonies that eventually became the United States of America and was available to every single person in those colonies.

Interestingly, Georgia, where I was being illegally detained, has played an influential role in the development of the Writ of Habeas Corpus, also known as the "Freedom Writ" and its original constitution was the first in US history to make access to the Writ a constitutional right.

In 1963, Justice William Brennan Jr. wrote that "government must always be accountable to the judiciary for a man's imprisonment." The prisoner is "entitled to his immediate release," the Justice emphasized, if the government violates the law in putting him behind bars. Brennan was one of the most influential justices of the 20th century. A champion of the individual versus the government—in what he called "the unceasing contest between personal liberty and government oppression"—he led the Supreme Court to strengthen American democracy by strengthening various roles of its citizens.

He embraced habeas corpus as part of that enhancement— as a crucial tool for the protection of constitutional rights. Following his lead, the Warren Court expanded habeas law to redress appalling treatment by many states of criminal defendants, especially minorities and the poor, who had often experienced unfair arrests, been coerced into confessions and received unjust trials.

Unfortunately, today, federal law governing habeas corpus makes it seem antique. The writ has withered and is in a shabby state. The Supreme Court occasionally lets petitions for writs go forward in federal courts, as it did this past term in a pair of 5-4 rulings. But far more often, the Court thwarts such intrusion, impatiently overturning federal appeals courts that have granted a state prisoner,for example, relief based on a habeas petition.

In the end, in my case, I wrote the Writ of Habeas Corpus "Olfemi Winter vs INS"(Case 6:03-cv-00014-WLS-GMF) in my own hand according to the law books I had been reading.

A habeas proceeding begins with the filing of a Verified Petition for the Writ. The petition must allege unlawful restraint, name the person by whom the petitioner is so restrained and specify the facts on which the petitioner bases his claim that the restraint is unlawful.

Generally, a habeas petition must allege:

the identity of the petitioner and thelocation of his custody;

the court order which led to the petitioner's restraint;

anillegal restraint on the petitioner's liberty;

why the petition is being filed in the appellatecourt;

there is no plain, speedy, and adequate remedy at law;

the legal claim for relief and the factual predicate;

no previous petition had been filed or why a successive petition should be permitted; and

in some cases, an allegation that the petition is timely or why delay is justified.

The petition must also include a prayer for relief and a verification. The document should contain points and authorities and exhibits.

I filed the Writ with the United States District Court for the Middle District of Georgia, Thomasville Division on March 12, 2003, Maxwell Wood being the United State Attorney for the Middle District of Georgia.

In The United State District Court
For the Middle District of Georgia
Thomasville Division

Olfemi Winter	x	
Petitioner	x	Civil Action File
	x	No. 6.03-CV-14(WLS
Vs	x	
	x	Habeas Corpus
Immigration and Nrtl. Service	x	28 U.S.C. 2241
	x	
Respondents.	x	

Petition For A Writ
Of Habeas Corpus

This is a petition for a writ of Habeas Corpus
filed before This Honorable Court because petitioner is
unlawfully detained in Violation of 28 U.S.C 2241,
and therefore he is entitled that this Honorable
Court issue a writ on his behalf directing the above
named Respondents (INS) to Release him from Custody
and in Support Therefor Petitioner Shows:

JURISDICTION

① This Court have absolute jurisdiction to grant
the Relief Requested Pursuant of 28 U.S.C 2241

-1-

44

I also filed a Motion for Stay of Deportation by the Immigration Service until my Writ of Habeas Corpus was adjudicated.

A Motion is a written request or proposal to the court to obtain an asked-for order, ruling or direction. In my case, I wanted to get an Order form the Court that prevented the Immigration Service from trying to deport me until my Writ of Habeas Corpus could be decided by a judge.

My resolve was supported by the Good Lord. On the 16th day after filing my Writ of Habeas Corpus I received a letter from the US District Court for the Middle District of Georgia, Thomasville Division. The Immigration Service had challenged my Writ of Habeas Corpus. The letter was the Judgment by the Court.

To my unmitigated surprise, US Magistrate Judge G. Mallon Faircloth found that the my Writ of Habeas Corpus

"does not appear subject to summary dismissal. WHEREFORE, the clerk of the Court is to issue summons for service by the US Marshal (upon) the United States (Immigration Service) (and) the United States Attorney is hereby order to show cause within a period not to exceed 60 days from the date of receipt of this Order, why this writ should not be granted."

IN THE UNITED STATES DISTRICT COURT
FOR THE MIDDLE DISTRICT OF GEORGIA
THOMASVILLE DIVISION

OLFEMI WINTER,

        Petitioner,

vs.

        CASE NO. 6:03-CV-14 (WLS)

IMMIGRATION and
NATURALIZATION
SERVICE,

        Respondent.

ORDER FOR SERVICE

Petitioner, OLEMI WINTER, has filed a pro se § 2241 petition for Habeas Corpus wherein he is challenging his continued detention by the Immigration and Naturalization Service (INS). Petitioner has paid the required filing fee.

IT IS DETERMINED that Petitioner's Motion challenging this detention does not appear subject to summary dismissal. WHEREFORE, the Clerk of the Court is to issue summonses for service by the U.S. Marshal; the U.S. Marshal is to serve the United States pursuant to Fed. R. Civ. P. 4(i)(1); and, pursuant to 28 U.S.C. § 2243, the United States Attorney is hereby Ordered to show cause, within a period not to exceed 60 days from the date of receipt of this Order, why the writ should not be granted.

SO ORDERED this 25th day of March 2003.

G. MALLON FAIRCLOTH
UNITED STATES MAGISTRATE JUDGE

ENTERED ON DOCKET
3.26.2003
Gregory J. Leonard, Clerk
Deputy Clerk

After my initial shout of joy in reading the decision, all the other detainees laughed at the grin on my face that just wouldn't go away! But they were happy for me and I greatly appreciated the support that was tacitly given me.

46

Some weeks after I filed the Writ, I was transported to the Immigration Center Offices in downtown Atlanta. I was put into a waiting room where I met two other Nigerian nationals who explained they were being deported. Maybe I was to be joining them. I was quite scared of that possibility. I knew the Service was still anxious to have me sent out of the United States.

In the end, I was transferred from the Immigration Center to Oakdale Federal Prison, New Orleans Parish, Louisiana.

I was escorted out of the Center in handcuffs and leg irons and led onto a bus with other immigration detainees and we drove the 470 miles to the Oakdale Federal Prison.

When I arrived there I telephoned the offices of Attorney Mobley to inquire if she knew why I was transported to the Immigration Center and what was going on. She "wasn't available" when I called and afterwards wouldn't take any of my calls.

But I was convinced and believe to this day that I wasn't being deported with the other Nigerians because of the Writ and Motion I had filed.

Later, through the courts, I found out why the Immigration Service transferred me out of Georgia.

Chapter 6

I WAS TRANSFERRED FROM GEORGIA to Louisiana. When I arrived at the New Orleans Parish Prison in Louisiana, one of the immigration officers said that they (the Immigration Service) would keep this up as long as I kept fighting them. But instead of intimidating me, it only strengthened my resolve!

But the Immigration Service wasn't so easily thwarted in their strategy to get me deported.

I received the Immigration Service's Answer to my Writ upon my arrival at the Louisiana Jail.

In his Answer to Judge Faircloth's Order to Show Cause, US Attorney Maxwell Wood through Assistant Attorney H. Randolph Aderhold reasoned in behalf of the Immigration Service as its primary argument in opposition to my Writ that, as I had been transferred from Colquitt County Jail in Georgia to the Oakdale Federal Prison in New Orleans Parish, Louisiana, the US District Court for the Middle District of Georgia, Thomasville Division no longer had jurisdiction over the case and therefore the Writ should be dismissed.

While a very sly and disingenuous tactic by the Immigration Service, technically under the law, they had a point.

But Judge Faircloth must have seen through their duplicitous attempt to side-step the law because instead of summarily dismissing the Writ as the Immigration Service had hoped, he ordered the action to be transferred to the United States District Court of the Eastern District of Louisiana, New Orleans Division.

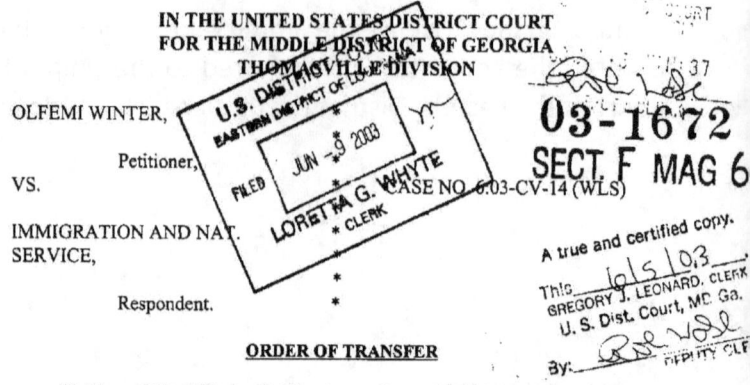

IN THE UNITED STATES DISTRICT COURT
FOR THE MIDDLE DISTRICT OF GEORGIA
THOMASVILLE DIVISION

OLFEMI WINTER,

        Petitioner,

VS.

IMMIGRATION AND NAT.
SERVICE,

        Respondent.

CASE NO. 6:03-CV-14 (WLS)

03-1672
SECT F MAG 6

A true and certified copy.

This 6 5 03
GREGORY J. LEONARD, CLERK
U. S. Dist. Court, MD. Ga.

By: _____
DEPUTY CLF

ORDER OF TRANSFER

    Petitioner, Olfemi Winter, filed the above referenced 28 U.S.C § 2241 action on March 12, 2003, while he was being detained at the Colquitt County Jail, Moultrie, Georgia, located in the Middle District of Georgia, Thomasville Division. Respondent has filed its Answer as ordered by this court. Respondent has shown this court that Petitioner has been transferred from the Colquitt County Jail to the Orleans Parish Prison, New Orleans, Louisiana. (Resp't Ex. A at ¶ 12). Therefore, since Petitioner is no longer detained in this district, the more appropriate jurisdiction of his habeas petition is the district where he is incarcerated. The Orleans Parish Prison is located in the Eastern District of Louisiana, New Orleans Division.

    THEREFORE, IT IS HEREBY ORDERED that Petitioner's habeas petition be transferred to the United States District Court of the Eastern District of Louisiana, New Orleans Division, 500 Camp Street, New Orleans, LA 70130.

    SO ORDERED this 4th day of June, 2003.

jsl

ENTERED ON DOCKET
6 5 2003
Gregory J. Leonard, Clerk
Deputy Clerk

G. MALLON FAIRCLOTH
UNITED STATES MAGISTRATE JUDGE

___ Fee_____
___ Process_____
_X_ Dktd £ßß
___ CtRmDep_____
___ Doc. No. _1_

What amazed me is that instead of addressing the issue about my detention and the legality of my being in the United States, the Immigration Service side-stepped the issue entirely,

50

costing US taxpayers large sums by keeping me detained, legal costs by the States Attorneys in two states, the hardship on me and my family and for what? To put off the core issues to another day and another Court, one perhaps more friendly to their objective of having me deported?

I could not help but wonder how many other detainees were in my very same position and how much it cost everyone in money, time and emotional cruelty.

But I was soon to discover this was the *modus operandi* of the Immigration Service, their pattern for handling matters.

Upon receipt of the transfer of "Olfemi Winter Vs INS"(Case 6:03-cv-00014-WLS-GMF)US District Judge Martin Feldman of the United States District Court of the Eastern District of Louisiana, New Orleans Division, also Ordered that the US Attorney for the Eastern District of Louisiana, the US Immigration and Naturalization Service and the US Attorney General file an Answer to my Writ explaining the government's position, including citations, within 30 days and assigned the case to Judge Louis Moore Jr.

Almost three weeks later, Kathryn W. Becnel, Assistant US Attorney, filed a motion for an additional 20 days extension of time.

UNITED STATES DISTRICT COURT
EASTERN DISTRICT OF LOUISIANA

OLEFMI WINTER,#44835, * CIVIL ACTION

   Plaintiff, * NUMBER: 03-1672

  v.   * SECTION: "F" (6)

IMMIGRATION AND   *
NATURALIZATION SERVICE,
         *
   Defendant.
     * * *

MOTION FOR EXTENSION OF TIME

NOW INTO COURT, through the undersigned Assistant United States Attorney, comes the defendant, The United States of America, who suggests to the court, pursuant to Rule 7.9E of the Uniform Local Rules, that he needs 20 additional days, up to and including August 6, 2003, in which to process, answer or otherwise plead.

DATE OF ENTRY

JUL 3 - 2003

- 1 -

I filed an Objection to the Motion. The Service had arbitrarily imprisoned me and kept me so detained and every day they held me was a day of my life that was lost forever. A day I could have worked, been with my family, enjoyed the simple acts of living free. Another day of a free life was being denied me!

So yes, I objected. And vehemently. In the end, however, the administrative procedure prevailed and the judge granted State Attorney Becnel her additional 20 days. Almost two months out of my life to file what should have been a simple Answer to a Writ to show why I was being detained.

But that was just a feint on the part of the Immigration Service.

I filed an Objection to Motion for Extension of Time based on the fact that there was no legal foundation for such an extension, the Immigration Service having been given 60days and another 30days to file an Answer already, an Answer which in fact had already been filed in the State of Georgia. So, they had more than enough time to prepare any remaining documents pertaining to the case. In my Objection I requested the judge dismiss the Motion for Extension of Time unless the Immigration Service came forward with a legal basis for need of such additional time.

In Addition to the Objection, I also filed a Motion for Appointment of Counsel to try and get some help in moving my case forward, some advice as how to better proceed both technically as well as strategically to have the *issues* of this case heard and addressed and not just spend time and effort on "technicalities". But, in the end, my Motion for Appointment of Counsel was denied.

Also, after recalling the Immigration Officer's comment about my being transferred as often as the Service deemed necessary, I also filed a Motion for a Temporary Restraining Order (TRO) to try and prevent the Immigration Service from transferring me yet again. For all the good it did me as in the end my Motion for a TRO was also denied!

Here is the government with all its money and legal personnel aligned against a self-taught (or rather self-learning) detainee. Talk about the odds being stacked against you! A modern day David and Goliath story!

However, the reason behind the Immigration Service's filing the Motion for Extension of Time now became apparent for the Service then went on to try and force my "voluntary deportation" described earlier, in the first chapter. Recall they had driven me to the Hartsfield–Jackson Atlanta International Airport and tried to force me onto the KLM flight to Nigeria via Amsterdam so that I could ask for asylum there.

On the one hand, their actions showed how scared the Service was becoming. On the other, from a different perspective, it showed how deceitful were their tactics in dealing with genuine issues under their mandate.

Chapter 7

AFTER THE ABORTED ATTEMPT by the Immigration Service to "voluntarily" deport me, I was taken from the Hartsfield–Jackson Atlanta International Airport to Etowah County Jail in Gadsden, AL.

The Etowah County Jail houses up to 350 immigration detainees who are awaiting disposition of their cases. Critics say conditions in the rural lockup are inhumane" and NBC News did a special report about the facility, noting how many of the detainees are in "limbo" there.

The report goes on to describe a number of detainees whose stores are similar to my own, including a detainee from Moldova who legally came to the US, married a US citizen, bought a house in Atlanta, GA and started a business. A clerical error, checking the wrong box on a driver's license application, resulted in his arrest a year and a half after the incident. Showing Immigration Office officers his green card and Moldavian passport showing his legal entry into the US availed him nothing and he was taken into custody.

He spent almost a year in jail, not knowing if he was going to be freed, deported or what. His marriage failed, he lost his house to foreclosure and his business imploded. When he was finally released, he returned to a shattered life. All because of a clerical error.

Such stories about the actions of the Immigration Service abound and genuinely reflect a system that is truly broken.

In my own case, when I arrived at the Etowah County Jail, I immediately wrote to the US District Court of the Eastern District of Louisiana to inform them of the Immigration Service's attempt

Ms Loretta Whyte
United State District Court
for The Eastern District of louisiana
500 Camp St, New Orleans LA.

U. S. DISTRICT COURT
Eastern District of Louisiana

FILED JUL 1 4 2003

LORETTA G. WHYTE
Clerk

RE: Olfemi Winter, Petitioner.
Vs
Immigration and Nat Serv, Respondents.
Case No 03-1672
Section "F" (6)

Dear Ms. Whyte

I pray that this letter meet you and the Honorable judge in good health.

Notwithstanding the pending Case at this Honorable Court and also the order of the honorable judge Martin L Feldman, the defendants (INS) illegally attempt to deport the petitioner mr. Winter. Petitioner was transfer to the Georgia airport on the 8 day of July 2003 for deportation. AT the Airport petitioner Show immigration officer C.T Davis, the order of the Honorable judge feldman and the motion for extension of time file by the US ATTorney Kathryn Becnel. Officer Davis Claim, nor the District Court of louisiana or the US ATTorney Becnel ever send the INS any order or notice of any kind.

___ Process
X Dktd
X CtRmDep
Doc. No.

Petitioner Olfemi Winter is presently incarcerated at ETOWAH COUNTY DETENTION CENTRE, 827 FORREST A

to force me into deportation with my case still open and not adjudicated, all contrary to law.

Assistant US Attorney Becnel now filed a Motion to Dismiss and included a Memorandum in Support of Motion. It was full of technical legal points but FAILED TO ADDRESS THE ISSUE OF MY DETENTION. The primary argument against my writ was the same in the Motion as in the Answer filed in Georgia- that I was no longer in the jurisdiction of the United States District Court for the Middle District of Georgia, Thomasville Division wherein the Writ was filed and therefore should be dismissed.

I had read in the newspapers during my time in the US before my detention about how criminals would get off "on a technicality". The argument by law enforcement was that justice wasn't being served and a guilty criminal was being set free not because he was innocent but because of an error, a technicality. The issues underlying the case were never addressed, and a guilty person was being released and free.

And here was the same situation but in reverse. Instead of a guilty man being set free on a technicality, here an innocent man continued being detained because of the technicality of jurisdiction. And this was a technicality that the Immigration Service in fact created, just in order to have the matter dismissed on that very technicality of jurisdiction!

UNITED STATES DISTRICT COURT
EASTERN DISTRICT OF LOUISIANA

FILED
U.S. DISTRICT COURT
EASTERN DISTRICT OF LA

2003 JUL 16 PM 3: 59

LORETTA G. WHYTE
CLERK

OLFEMI WINTER	*	CIVIL ACTION
	*	NUMBER: 03-1672
v.	*	SECTION: "F" (6)
IMMIGRATION AND NATURALIZATION SERVICE	*	

*   *   *

MOTION TO DISMISS

NOW INTO COURT, through the undersigned Assistant United States Attorney, comes the United States of America and respectfully moves this Honorable Court to dismiss the claim of Olfemi Winter for lack of subject matter jurisdiction.

Respectfully submitted,

JIM LETTEN
UNITED STATES ATTORNEY

KATHRYN W. BECNEL (23641)
Assistant United States Attorney
Hale Boggs Federal Building
501 Magazine Street, Second Floor
New Orleans, Louisiana 70130
Telephone: (504) 680-3025

Fee____
Process____
X Dktd____
CtRmDep____
Doc. No.____

It's as wrong here as when a guilty criminal can get away with a crime because of such technicalities. It makes no difference and law enforcement can't have it both ways!

While I understood the basic principles of immigration law, I lacked any real experience in the law. I was essentially learning as

58

I went along, which meant mistakes and errors that hurt me instead of aiding my case. And, while I understood English, I missed many nuances in the language of the law that also hurt me.

I also did one other thing. I called the Nigerian Embassy.

Under Nigerian law, a travel document is required in order to enter the Nigeria. I had never filed for a travel document, so I was curious as to how the Immigration Service had received one when they tried to have me boarded onto that KLM flight.

The Embassy informed me that they, as a matter of course, automatically issued a travel document in the name of a Nigerian national if requested by the Immigration Service as part of their deportation proceedings.

I took issue with the Embassy as there was no investigation into the matter and no determination as to whether I was being deported legally or illegally, whether I am a Nigerian citizen, whether there was an open case waiting to be adjudicated, or what was the situation at all. At the very least, they could have interviewed me.

Additionally, a request for travel document had to have my photo and signature. I never provided either. I did discover that the Immigration Service used a photo of me naked when I was first brought into detention as the required photo. I asked them if they didn't think it odd that a photo of me naked to be used for a travel document perhaps warranted some question or investigation on their part?

I asked for the Embassy's assistance and intervention after I explained my situation to them but they asserted a lack of jurisdiction in such immigration matters.

To the Embassy's credit though, approximately a week into my detention at Etowah, in Alabama, they telephoned to interview me.

We reviewed my case together and they advised the Immigration Service that they would only accept a current head shot photo and signature for any travel document for me in the future.

To put such a photo and signature into my file, the Immigration Service brought me into an interview room, handcuffed me to a chair and tried to take a headshot photo. I refused to cooperate and the officer grabbed me by the jaw to try to force a pose in order for them to snap a photo.

There was a bit of a tussle as I would not cooperate. As punishment, they ordered me put in "the hole" at the Jail. But when the attending jail guard asked the reason "for the record" the Service couldn't well explain why. Up to that point I was a "model prisoner" offering no trouble or problem. As a result, I was put in solitary for one or two weeks and then sent back into the general population.

In large part this is due to guards maintaining the misconception that immigration detention is meant to be penal, a punishment for some illegality.

It is however most certainly not penal. There is no crime that detainees have been convicted of and in many cases, such as my own, detainees are detained without basis, without cause, which in no way can be construed as criminal.

One of the more interesting events that occurred close to the end of my initial tenure in Alabama was a visit by a Congressional Inspection team. They were acting as prisoner and detainee advocacy panel, investigating living conditions and listing grievances and complaints.

The team was overwhelmed with the grievances and complaints from both groups, prisoners and detainees. There was much shouting as this was one of the few opportunities we all had to air our complaints.

All of the commotion associated with the inspection resulted in a general lockdown of the facility wherein we were shut into our cells for 23 out of 24 hours a day.

There was no reason for this and certainly not amongst the detainees who were not classified as prisoners.

I helped organize a hunger strike amongst the detainees to protest our treatment and the lockdown, which lasted some four days.

During my time in the law library, I had discovered the sections in the law that differentiated our status as detainees from prisoners serving sentences. When the negotiators finally arrived, I explained these differences and how we as detainees we were not subject to the same lockdown response or actions as the general prisoner population. Again, it was the mistaken belief that detainees were there for penal (criminal) reasons and not because they were waiting for disposition.

To their credit, the negotiators reviewed my findings and agreed with us! From that point on we were treated according to the regulations for detainees and not those addressing prisoners.

Chapter 8

I WAS AGAIN TRANSPORTED to the Immigration Center in Atlanta, GA. I was in the basement holding area again, handcuffed to a chair.

An Immigration Service officer came in and again requested I submit for a photograph and signature or at least a thumb print to verify identification and acquiescence to Nigerian travel documents.

I calmly re-iterated that until my case was adjudicated, I would not submit to a photograph, signature or fingerprint. I explained that if my case was decided and an Order of Deportation issued by the Court I would so submit. As he could not produce such an Order I was within my rights to refuse.

He left and went to talk with his superior. When he returned he came back with an additional six or seven officers. "Uh, oh, here it comes" I thought to myself.

And I was right. Two officers grabbed my legs, and another and two grabbed my arm, while a third held my head. Another one tried to force my hand open and pry a finger out to force my fingerprint onto a travel document request. I fought against all their efforts. So one of the guards holding my legs grabbed me by the testicles and squeezed. The pain was excruciating but still I fought their efforts.

In the end, the document became so smudged as to be useless. Rather than get another completed copy, the officers just gave up.

After this fiasco, I was transported back to Alabama.

My return heralded a flurry of activity. Assistant US Attorney Karen Becnel had filed a Motion to Dismiss with the Louisiana Court for "lack of subject matter jurisdiction". She included a ten page Memorandum in Support which highlighted all of the technical points of law and case law why my Writ of Habeas Corpus should be dismissed for lack of jurisdiction. NOWHERE DID IT EVER ADDRESS THE WRONGFUL ISSUE OF MY DETENTION.

Nor was it ever pointed out that I was removed from the jurisdiction of the Court in I which I filed my Write by the Immigration Service itself, in order to sidestep the very point of the Writ- to have the Immigration Service explain to the Court why I was being detained in the first place.

In the end, Judge Louis Moore Jr., the US District Court Judge for the US District Court, Eastern District of Louisiana, found that it didn't have jurisdiction as the Writ was filed in the State of Georgia. He granted the Immigration Service's Motion to Dismiss.

Unlike Judge Faircloth in Georgia, who saw through the machinations of the Immigration Service and instead ordered the matter transferred to the US District Court in Eastern Louisiana where I had been transferred, and as I had been transferred from Louisiana to Alabama, Judge Louis Moore Jr. should have been transferred the case to the US District Court for the Northern District of Alabama and the Motion to Dismiss not ruled upon by him. It follows the same logic as the US Attorney was making. If the US District Court Judge for Georgia was jurisdictionally unable to render a judgment because of my transfer out of his District, so too the US District Court Judge for Louisiana should have been jurisdictionally unable to render a judgment as I had been transferred to Alabama!

There is also the concept in law known as "in the interest of justice". Unfortunately, it's a concept that gains little traction these days. As was so succinctly said about our Court system, "we are not a Court of justice but a Court of laws." Unfortunately law without justice can be twisted to suit one's needs for as Justice Earl Warren said "It is the spirit and not the form of law that keeps justice alive".

So, knowing my days were numbered, even though I was still in pain from the actions of the Immigration officers in Atlanta, I filed or followed up on previous filings that included an Objection to Motion to Dismiss, a Motion to Procure an Order against Immigration Officer Terry Michael to prevent him from using excessive force against me I re-filed a Motion for Bond and finally I filed a Motion for Default Judgment based upon the material in my original Writ of Habeas Corpus, the use of force by the Immigration Service against me and failure by the Service to provide an Answer to my Writ in a timely fashion.

IN THE UNITED STATE DISTRICT COURT
EASTERN DISTRICT OF LOUISIANA

Olfemi Winter
Petitioner   : Civil Action file
                                        : NO 03-1672
Vs   : Section F (6)

Immigration and Nat   : Habeas   Corpus
Service, et al   : 28 U.S.C 2241
Respondents

MOTION FOR DEFAULT JUDGMENT

        Petitioner Olfemi Winter Respectfully urges the Court
enter a default judgment in this Case because the
Respondents did not appear and file a response in a timely
fashion, and it requested for a Continuation in a malicious
and arbitrary fashion to give the opportunity to immigration
authority to use unnecessary and excessive force
Seeking the deportation of the petitioner while this
Case Still pending.

        The ground for this Motion at issue are more
particularly described in the attached Declaration.

Wherefore, Petitioner pray that If an answer

65

There had been a hearing set for the Assistant State Attorney Karen Becnel's Motion to Dismiss and I wanted to get as many of my own motions and supporting evidence before the Court as possible before that hearing.

As the hearing was in Louisiana and I was in Alabama, I called the Court in Louisiana to inquire about the need for my presence. After all, the attorney I had hired, Attorney Barbara Mobley failed in her representation of me and wouldn't even take my calls, I was without funds to hire another attorney privately, my Motion to have counsel assigned was denied, I was acting *Pro Se*, that is, representing myself, in a system of which I was only scratching the surface in understanding or being able to adequately and correctly apply, and I was in another State, intentionally transported there to facilitate the Immigration Service's failure to admit to their error and denying me my liberty.

The Court Clerk in the US District court for Louisiana for the Eastern District, immediately recognized my name when I called. As I was acting Pro Se, I needed to know how I could be present for the hearing. The Clerk informed me it wasn't necessary for me to be present, that the judge could rule with my being *in absensia,* that is, in my physical absence.

To say I was despondent after the call would be a significant understatement. How could I have my "day in Court" if the Court wouldn't even allow me to be there to argue my case?

I filed a Motion for an Order of Transfer that I might be transferred to Louisiana to be able to attend the hearing in person.

IN THE UNITED STATE DISTRICT COURT

FOR THE EASTERN DISTRICT OF LOUISIANA

Olpemi Winter

Petitioner

Us

Immigration and Nat
Service, et al
Respondents

Civil Action file

No: 03 - 1672

Section F (6)

Habeas Corpus

28 U.S.C 2241

MOTION TO PROCURE AN ORDER

TO BE RETURN TO LOUISIANA

Petitioner Olpemi Winter Respectfully urges the Court
order the Respondent's to return the petitioner to lousiana.

The grounds for this motion at issue are more
particularly described in attached Declaration
of Olpemi Winter.

Wherefore, petitioner pray this Court grant
relief as a matter of due process, and equal
justice of law, an order petitioner be
lousiana,

Fee ____
____ Process ____
X Dktd ____
X CtRmDep ____
Doc. No. ____

67

At the end of the day, none of my motions were granted, I was not present for my hearing and Judge Louis Moore Jr. ruled in favor of the Immigration Service and ordered my Writ of Habeas Corpus dismissed on the grounds of lack of jurisdiction.

MINUTE ENTRY
FELDMAN, J.
August 25, 2003

FILED
U.S. DISTRICT COURT
EASTERN DISTRICT OF LA

2003 AUG 26 AM 10: 18

LORETTA G. WHYTE
CLERK

UNITED STATES DISTRICT COURT

EASTERN DISTRICT OF LOUISIANA

OLFEMI WINTER   *   CIVIL ACTION

VERSUS   *   NO. 03-1672

IMMIGRATION AND   *   SECTION "F"
NATURALIZATION SERVICE

Before the Court is the government's motion to dismiss for
lack of jurisdiction. The government asserts that the Court
does not have jurisdiction over the plaintiff's Writ of Habeas
Corpus because at the time the petition was filed, neither
plaintiff nor his custodian was located in this judicial
district. The Court agrees. When plaintiff filed his petition
he was physically within the Middle District of Georgia and his
custodian, the Assistant District Director for Detention and
Removal for the Atlanta District of the Department of Homeland
Security, was within the jurisdiction of the United States
District Court for the Middle District of Georgia. Thus, the
Court does not have jurisdiction. See Montalban v. Bureau of
Immigration and Customs Enforcement, et al., No. 03-760 (E.D.
La. May 30, 2003)(citing Vasquez v. Reno, 233 F.3d 688 (1st Cir.
2000), cert. denied, 534 U.S. 816, 122 S.Ct. 43(2001)).

___ Fee_____
_X_ Process _____
___ Dktd _____
___ CtRmDep _____
___ Doc. No. _____

DATE OF ENTRY

AUG 2 6 2003

I considered this a genuine travesty of justice. The
Immigration Service did everything in its power to thwart review
of the facts of my case, that I was legally in the US and married to

a Permanent US Resident as attested to by previous Immigration Service documents, about my improper and illegal detention and a decision based upon the facts, all at a major cost to the taxpayers of this country.

Had they been straightforward this matter could have been reviewed and decided in one week. I didn't care about the abuse I had endured. I just wanted to go back to my family and live a normal life, as I had been living before my arrest and detention.

I knew from my reading that I had only 30 days to appeal. I quickly drafted a Response to the Order regarding Motion to Dismiss highlighting the Immigration Service's attempt to side-step the law by their "mistaken" attempt to deport where the merits of my case as outlined in the Writ could not be judged and how they were now free to again attempt to deport me, though they had no legal basis to do so.

I began preparing my Appeal. But the Immigration Service had other ideas.

Chapter 9

IN THE MIDST OF MY APPEAL preparation I was transferred to Texas. To this day I do not know where.

But between the travel, the break in preparing the Appeal and access to legal resources, the time limit passed and I lost my right to Appeal.

That's all the Immigration Service needed. All of their subsequent actions were intended to merely "run out the clock" on the time I had to lodge my appeal.

I was in Texas only a relatively short period before I was transferred yet again, first back to another state jail where I was boarded onto a plane and then moved to some place on the US-Canadian border.

I was only there for a matter of 48hours before being told I was being deported. But how could that be I asked? I had an open case. I was never made aware of a decision for my deportation having been ordered or otherwise rendered.

I was boarded onto a flight to Lagos, along with a number of other deportees. A representative of the Nigerian Embassy was on hand to record our disposition and provide the necessary travel documents.

I had with me a small bag with some clothes in it. No money on me or in an account somewhere.

I wasn't able to call anyone in Lagos to tell them I was returning. But the worst was not being able to call my wife and tell her I was being deported. To say good-bye to her and to my children. To tell her I would keep fighting to return to the United States to be with her and our family. That was heartache almost unbearable.

I remember it was dark on the flight as it was a night flight. Not a pitch black darkness, as the plane's cabin lights were turned down low and no overhead lights were on.

Even though it was dark, I couldn't sleep. There were too many emotions running around in my gut to sleep. Anger, Depression. Even fear.

There were a little more than a dozens of us, all being deported back to Lagos.

Ten years I had been living in the United States. Ten years trying to do the right thing, work through the immigration system to legally remain here. Thwarted by the very system created to provide a mechanism for allowing the immigration of foreign nationals. Physically beaten, Nearly choked to death. Cheated by lawyers who took my money and then never fulfilled their legal obligations to me. Moved from jail to jail and Prison so that my case couldn't be adjudicated on its merits, but by creating a situation where the case could be decided on a technicality, All in an effort to wear me down with this single, ultimate objective- to have me deported and hide the embarrassment of the actions made by officers of the Immigration Service.

But that wasn't the worst of it. The worst of it was being ripped away from my wife and children. By all I knew of US immigration law, there was no way I should have been deported. Yet, there I was, in handcuffs and ankle restraints, on the way to Lagos. I missed my family. And that depressed me greatly.

I wondered what it would be like in Lagos now. Always a tumultuous country, it was never more evident than in this large and fast growing city. Things were bad. Corruption and nepotism in past governments were rife. As a young man and an idealist, I had believed things could be made better, which is why I had become involved in politics in the first place.

And, if I wanted to continue to live, why I ultimately had to flee the country in the first place.

And now I was back. What would the country be like? Would I be arrested upon my arrival? What would my family there think? And what about my family back in the US? What would happen to them without me?

So many questions.So few answers.

Chapter 10

ONE OF THE OTHER DEPORTEES I returned with was being met at the airport. I hitched a ride with him into town where I called my sister 'xola'. I gave her the sad news of my arrival and asked her to come get me.

But the first thing I really needed to do was to call and tell my family what happened.

I was worried about the effect my deportation would have on my parents so I stayed with my sister until I could get my legs under me, so to speak.

Everything was different in Nigeria. After all, it had been 10 years. Luckily, the government had changed and I needn't be afraid of repercussions from my original political involvements so long ago.

I remember the next day after my arrival I went to the Embassy. I just stood in front of the building looking at it, thinking. My standing there must have aroused suspicion because first a plainclothes security officer and then a uniformed police officer approached to ask me what I was doing there. In this day and age, I couldn't blame them for being suspicious.

Eventually, I started to come out of it, at least to some degree, enough to become functional again.

I knew that once deported, the likelihood of being allowed back into the United States was slim. But I had to try. What other choice did I have? I wanted to be with my family!

So, I contacted my wife and asked her to get another attorney. About a month later she found an attorney in Georgia who specialized in immigration law, a Mr. Charles Kurt. Attorney Kurt was one of two attorneys who showed competence and integrity, the other being my attorney in New York City, Moses Apsan.

Attorney Kurt explained I really had only one option available and that was to follow-up on the filing for immigration as the spouse of an American citizen.

I paid him his retainer. He explained it might "take a while", to "hang in there" and that he would get back to me when he knew something.

It took seven years for him to be able to get back to me!

Chapter 11

AFTER ABOUT A MONTH, I moved out of my sister's house and moved back in with my parents.

They took it hard when I told them I had been deported. My mother was in hysterics and my father, normally very staid, was visibly upset. They were most concerned for my family.

Their advice to me was most impactful. As we were a Christian family and my parents were both very religious, their counsel for me was to continue to pray and to fast, to have faith and then I would be victorious in the end. Their advice was both sustaining and prophetic.

The emotional paralysis I had been suffering from the PTSD began to lessen. But it was still hard. I often called my family and it broke my heart each and every time when my son said "Daddy, I want you to come home". He kept on asking for three years and it just tore me up.

I also knew that I had to start earning money. At the time, the IT industry was just beginning in Nigeria. Because of my IT background and the computer skill set I had acquired, I began to consult with a number of IT service providers and directly with companies who were in need of IT services.

I began working with a man who was putting together a proposal for the government in the state of Lagos to computerize the state's pension system. The proposal was well received and the IT model we developed was adopted.

This was the beginning of a number of assignments in the private sector upon which I consulted, some smaller, some quite extensive. One in particular, Tetrazzini Plc, had a few projects for me. My skill set in IT networking systems and database administration were less available than web design or system administration and so I had found a niche.

I also saw an opportunity with a company in Italy, Orisline, which had created software for dental practices and dental laboratories. I struck a deal to represent them in Nigeria. For every software package sold in the country I was contracted for its installation. This was especially important for clinics with multiple sites as I would network each branch.

In the end, I set up my own consulting company in Nigeria, Global Computer, Ltd., as I had a good reputation as a problem solver in IT networking and database administration and for good work at a reasonable price.

About six years into my return stay in Nigeria, my experience and reputation was such that I was offered a trip to China to attend a series of training workshops in Shanghai.

I studied basic Mandarin Chinese so I could at least get around and, while I was there for only a week, I visited Shanghai and the industrial zone in Guangzhou.

The irony of my being allowed into China, a Communist regime where everyone's activities are monitored and recorded but being deported from the United States, the proverbial land of the free and land of opportunity, was not lost upon me.

Even though I was making a living, my actual wages based on a Western scale were still relatively insignificant. Nevertheless, I sent whatever money I could to my wife to help support her and the children.

Yet, through it all, I could never shake off the betrayal of the US immigration system and the divide they caused in my family, all without need or cause. To this day I cannot understand the reasoning of the Immigration Service, other than the belief that the best way to treat immigration was by deportation.

I was and am a skilled professional, without a criminal record, who was never a terrorist, who could and did contribute to society by working, raising a family, paying taxes, helping people where I could. Why penalize and deport someone like me without any genuine cause? I could understand if I were a drug dealer or robbed and beat people. That is after all from what the Immigration Service should be protecting society. But I wasn't in that category.

So why? And the argument that I just "fell through the cracks" doesn't hold because there are too many people exactly like me who suffered the outrageousness of illegal and immoral deportation.

Later, I read about how many others had been "rounded up" by the Immigration Service as "criminals", like a pastor in Iowa who was arrested and was awaiting deportation because he was arrested for Driving Under the Influence of alcohol (DUI) 17 years previously. Why wasn't he deported at the time? Why, after 17 years when he had married, trained and was ordained a minister, married with four children, was he deemed a "threat" and subject to deportation.

Nobody denies the Immigration Service is legally bound to deport criminals, but what they consider "criminal" and their timing suggests something radically wrong with the understanding of that mission.

I recalled my plight and how I missed my family every single day of my time in Nigeria. At the end of the day, I would have given up everything I had realized there if I could just go back and be with my family.

Chapter 12

NINE YEARS. IT TOOK SEVEN years for attorney Charles Kurt to push through my application for immigration based upon my being married to my wife and another two years before I received my visa and green card approval.

Nine years waiting and praying for the opportunity to return to the United States.

But those nine years had taken their toll. Both upon me and upon my family. In those intervening years, my wife and I grew apart. I couldn't blame her, holding on and never knowing if I would ever be allowed to return to her and our family.

So you can imagine how I was completely taken by surprise when I received an email from attorney Charles Kurt seven years after I had originally retained him. He wrote that my application was approved, congratulated me and that I should proceed to the US Embassy Consular Division in Lagos for my interview for my visa! No fireworks, no fanfare. Except for my jumping up and down when I read the email!

I called my family in the United States. I was only able to speak with my daughter and told her Daddy was finally coming home!

I then told my parents. They all jumped up and down along with me, glad that I had been vindicated and that my efforts were finally successful!

A date had already been scheduled for the interview when the application was approved. When I arrived with the acceptance letter and all my other documents in hand, the Consular representative went through my entire case. After I finished and she reviewed the documents, the interviewer couldn't understand why I had been deported in the first place. She asked a myriad of questions. Did I commit any crime? I told I never committed any crime either here in Nigeria, nor in the United States. Why was I sent back? I explained I didn't understand myself why. She seemed to genuinely sympathize with me.

Generally, a deportee is prohibited from re-entering the United States for a period of time after his or her deportation. The period ranges anywhere from one to ten years or more depending upon a number of variables.

The interviewer asked how long a waiting period I was decreed. I answered her that I was not aware that there even was such a required waiting period or that a decreed waiting period had been put into my record. She requested I go home, think about it and try to recall any details about a waiting period while she looked through the records available to her.

Two days later the Consulate called and asked me to come back in. When I arrived, the same Interviewer said she couldn't find any such record either and recommended I apply for a waiver, just in case there was a waiting period declaration hidden away in some file somewhere. Otherwise there could be another "technicality" by which I could later be deported yet again!

The Interviewer seemed to empathize so much with my plight that I was genuinely moved by her compassion.

I thanked her profusely for her advice and counsel.

I wrote out an affidavit in support of the waiver and filed the application for waiver through my lawyer. I knew it would take some time for the waiver to be processed. Indeed, it took another full year for the review to be completed and the waiver granted.

So, I continued as before, with a number of work-related consulting assignments that needed my attention.

But I felt rewarded and that in the end I would prevail. My sense of hope was renewed and I was suffused with new strength and commitment to see this through. There was light at the end of the tunnel!

It was hard waiting but after all I'd been through I wasn't about to give up now.

I received another email from my attorney again congratulating me on the approval for the waiver. I was overjoyed and called the Consulate to see what was next.

I was informed that the Consulate had not yet received a copy of the waiver. Knowing that all immigration documentation was processed the US Immigration Processing Center in Ghana, I called the Center to try and get an update. They informed me that they had received the waiver approval and forwarded the notification to the Consulate in Lagos.

I waited a month before I called the Consulate again and was informed they had still not received a copy of the approval. I was frustrated with this bureaucracy and called the Ghana processing center a second time. They only confirmed that the approval had indeed been forwarded to the Consulate.

It was several months 'seven months' afterward that I was contacted by the Consulate that they had finally received the waiver approval letter.

It totaled about a year before I received final approval for immigration and was notified to come to the Consulate to have the visa entered into my passport.

The final steps were a breeze and before I knew it, I was looking at my fresh, shiny visa that would let me back into the United States!

It was a long and trying process but I did it and legally too. All my life I had been doing things the right way, the moral and legal way, so as not to get up caught-up in the traps of falsehood and deceit. Those kinds of immoral actions inevitably lead to one's downfall.

And while I suffered much, I was vindicated in the end and could return with my head held high!

Chapter 13

AS I MENTIONED ABOVE, IT was still in its infancy in Nigeria. I worked hard but didn't make a lot of money. Enough to make ends meet. Still, it had the added benefit of keeping busy so as not to go crazy. Not that that worked all the time either.

I have to confess to a period of darkness during this time in Nigeria where I contemplated suicide. It was all just too overwhelming for me. To know that I had a family waiting for me, that I was deported without merit from the country where my family was living and not knowing if I would ever be able to see them again finally got to be too much for me. In Nigeria I wasn't thriving, just surviving. And my memories were causing a sense of severe desperation even unto my very soul.

I kept asking what was the point of it all? After what I had been through, all the suffering, was it all worth it? The worst of course was simply not knowing if I would ever see my family again. It was like I was in a haze. A miasma of desperation and remorse.

I'd even gone so far as to write a suicide note, explaining that I felt I had nothing to look forward to and felt there was no way out of my situation.

But God in His Infinite Mercy saw my suffering and at this moment of the greatest darkness of my soul, shone a beacon of light.

It came in the form of a telephone call from the daughter of one of my best friends. Her name was Rejoice and she was only 8 or 9 at the time. To this day I remember her saying "Uncle Femi (as Uncle was a term of endearment between close family friends in Nigeria) 'I will punish you' (if you do it). How could she know what I was contemplating? But her words brought a smile to my face and I remembered my own daughter only about a year old when I was detained and deported. I remembered her smiling at me and kissing me on the cheek as she wrapped her tiny arms around my neck.

And it was as if the fog in my brain lifted. Just like that and God re-instilled in me a sense of hope. It was after all, hope that sustained me, upon which I could believe that, in the end, I would prevail.

If it weren't for the Lord's intercession through this little child, I would be dead now and only the Evil One would have prevailed during this Dark Night of the Soul.

It was not long after that when I heard from my attorney that my immigration application had been approved and I was to go to the US Consulate for the visa interview.

I guess it's true what they say that when you hit rock bottom, the only way to go is up!

I survived the seemingly bottomless pit that was my depression, successfully overcame all the obstacles to getting a waiver and ultimately my visa and Green Card approval and felt the lightness of vindication in my heart.

All that remained was getting back to the United States! I called my family to give them the good news that I had received my visa and permanent residency status and that I was coming home!

My big brother and his wife Mr. and Mrs. Olatunbobe, knowing that my finances were tight, purchased my ticket for me and gave me some extra cash for the trip as well. I packed some clothes, documents and assorted items and about a week later, left for Murtala Muhammed International Airport in Ikeja, Lagos to board a Delta flight to Atlanta, Georgia.

I remember watching people drop off friends with their families, wishing that it were me with my family. I remember being in line at the Airport to get my boarding pass, wondering if my family would be at the airport waiting for me. While I was very excited it was also very emotional for me, yet again not knowing what was ahead of me.

But these trying times had, in the end, made me stronger and, after enduring all that I had over the intervening years, I knew I could survive almost anything.

After going through security I was in the waiting lounge waiting to board the flight when I saw an old friend. He was visiting Nigeria but lived in Atlanta with his family and was flying home.

We chatted for a while and while he knew about my deportation, propriety kept him asking what my situation was currently. Still, he left to make a call and returned with a big smile upon his face. He'd obviously been able to somehow determine that I had won my case and was returning to the US legitimately.

They began boarding the flight and we each took our seat. Next to me sat a woman with a one year girl, the rest of her family in surrounding seats.

I mentioned to the woman that the last time I saw my daughter she was about her daughter's age. I quickly added that I was in Nigeria taking care of a few matters and was flying home to my family after a somewhat extended period to forestall any deeper inquiries as to why I hadn't seen my own daughter for some time. After all, my daughter was now about 10 and, at the time, it was just too personal and too painful to explain what had happened to me.

It led me to wonder if my son and daughter would recognize me, even acknowledge me as their father as I'd been away for the greater part of their lives.

That weighed heavy on my heart.

I was going home in the fullest sense of the word. I felt like the prodigal son returning, even though I hadn't left my home willingly as had the prodigal son in the Bible story.

I could only hope for a joyful return. Alas, in the intervening nine years that I'd been away, some things had changed that were beyond repair.

Chapter 14

WE ARRIVED IN ATLANTA about 6:00 in the morning after a 12 hour flight.

I was arriving with my own passport, in my own name and with a genuine visa. I had made it! I was victorious in overcoming the forces that would keep me from my family, that tore me from them unjustly and without cause.

Still, I had to admit to a certain trepidation when I approached the Immigration Officer at Border and Immigration Control, especially after he asked me to follow him!

He led me to a counter behind the admittance kiosks, along with several other people. To my relief, it was only to assist in processing my green card and review the package of documents I'd received from the Consulate in Lagos.

When asked where I would be living, I gave them my family's address in Atlanta. They gave me another package of documents including guidelines for new green card holders.

My friend saw me at the table and asked what was going on? I didn't want to get into it and just asked him to wait for me "on the other side".

I exited Border and Immigration Control and looked for my family amongst those waiting to receive arriving passengers.

To my bitter disappointment, I didn't see them. My heart ached that after overcoming so many hurdles to get back to them, my family was nowhere in sight.

I found my friend and he was good enough to take me home with him to rest and give me the opportunity to get hold of my family. After we arrived and I had a chance to freshen up a little, I took a cab to the address I had for my family. Maybe they got the day or time wrong. Won't they be surprised and happy to finally see me!

I looked at the listing of apartment residents by the door but didn't see my family's name. I looked up the manager and asked her about my family. Maybe I had misunderstood the section or they moved to a different unit.

The manager remembered the name but my heart sank when he told they had moved out some time ago. I was decimated and took the cab back to my friend's home.

Once there I telephoned my wife using the number I had for her. I told her I was back and in Atlanta. She was rather cool in her conversation with me, not excited as I had expected my arrival would cause her to be. We chatted on for a moment and she asked where I was staying. We agreed to meet at my friend's home the next day. She would bring the children with her.

I was desperate to know what was going on and though I needed to rest after the long flight, my emotional exhaustion caused me to be "overtired" and I rested only fitfully while I waited for my family to arrive.

The next day couldn't come soon enough for me but I finally saw my wife arrive. It was raining and another young woman held an umbrella for her and my wife. I couldn't figure out who my wife brought with her, though I did see my son accompanying them.

When they came inside I realized the young woman was my daughter whom I hadn't seen since she was one year old!

Indeed, both my children had grown so very much. My only connection with them was by telephone so I was left with only my old memories of how they looked.

There was an emotional undercurrent however, a straining that was most evident in my wife.

She made it clear to me that she "wasn't ready" to have me come home with them. I was taken aback. Ten years wasn't enough to "get ready"? But I didn't want to start off my return with an argument or show some kind of attitude, especially in front of the kids. I guess I choked on my emotions a bit, but agreed we should take it slow.

It was also interesting to note that my children seemed to already know that Daddy wouldn't be going home with them. I told them that everything would be alright. I knew inside that I was a survivor, after all that I'd been through, and that I would survive this too.

But there were the needs of daily living to attend to, especially in light of the fact that I wouldn't be living with my family, at least for the foreseeable future. And I knew I couldn't impose on my friend for much longer.

So, my priorities included a job and a place to live.

I'd always had a good relationship with my in-laws and so took a shot and called my mother-in-law, thinking maybe she would let me stay a few days until I could get myself organized. She was very happy to hear from me and congratulated me on my official return and green card status. She readily agreed to let me stay with her until I could get back on my feet.

I was in a bit of a bind because I had given my wife's old address as my US address for purposes of receiving my green card in the mail. I obviously wasn't there and so called Immigration Services to advise them of my new address.

I stayed with my mother-in-law for about three weeks during which time I received my green card and could now prove that I could legally work in the United States.

I found a menial job but at least it was something! The pay was trifle but it was a start.

Through someone I knew at my church I found out about a basement apartment that was available and within my new means.

I knew I was starting over again but it didn't matter. I had read about the newly immigrated from Eastern Europe for example, many who were physicians or had advanced degrees and who also mopped floors or had other such menial jobs when they arrived. I knew how they felt. Like them, I just swallowed my pride and did what I had to do. To adapt is to survive!

My wife remained distant and non-committal. My mother-in-law refused to get in the middle of things between her daughter and me, which I both understood and believed to be the right course of action for her. This was a problem between my wife and myself and I am forever grateful to her that, even in the midst of this chaos, she found it in her heart to help me.

I came to understand however, that my wife, out of necessity, had moved on even if it was a decision she made in her own mind. She had a husband whom she didn't know would ever come back to her and two children to worry about. Out of necessity, both psychological and from the needs of day-to-day living, she was obliged to create a new life for herself and the children, one that didn't include me.

Understanding it didn't make it any easier on me though. I had been so obsessed with getting back to my family that I had never envisioned the possibility that we wouldn't all be happily together again.

But she didn't prevent me from seeing my children, though that too had its problems.

I remember when I first got my basement apartment I had the kids come and stay the night. When they arrived and after the pleasantries were concluded, it became awkward as we tried to find common ground. My son evidently wanted to talk but to my daughter I was a complete stranger. That base of family love and daily interaction was missing and I lacked the parenting skills and the familiarity that comes through such interactions. I felt so lost that I excused myself for a moment and went outside to call a friend on my cell phone and ask him for advice about what I should do.

My daughter became bored and went to sleep early while I recalled with my son times we had spent doing things together. Like the time we were driving together in a parking, he handling the steering wheel while sitting on my lap. He was at that age when driving was first thing on his mind and so a week later I helped him get his driver's permit.

In the end, I was just happy we could spend the time together.

But it was still hard. I was only making a little per hour, had to pay rent, utilities, food, etc. There just wasn't much left over and I couldn't often buy my kids a present or give them pocket money.

Still, I continued to see my children, albeit sporadically. We would go shopping or for walks, to fast-food restaurants- the few things that I could afford to do with them.

My return was bittersweet for me as our times together were strained. We continued to be strangers to one another. And the relationship with my wife was not developing. While I voluntarily paid her child support, it was limited at best, my providing what I could from my meager earnings. Money issues plagued our relationship and drove us further apart. It caused me lots of heartache but there was little I could do about it.

The relationship was entirely different now. For me, that relationship had stopped at a specific point in time, when I was detained and ultimately deported.

For me, time froze. My wife and children remained static, though in reality life for them went on, just without me.

I was reminded of a Tom Hanks movie called Castaway. After being stranded on a desert island for several years after a plane crash and being sustained on that island by the memory of his fiancée, Hanks is finally rescued. But in the interim, his fiancée has mourned and buried him, ultimately moving on with her life and had even gotten married. While he knew intellectually that was likely going to be the case, in his heart time had stopped and his return was to that very point in time when he left.

It was the same with me. But, just like with Tom Hanks in the movie, time marches on, and things were not like either of us had expected.

In fact, things had continued to deteriorate. I'd been in Atlanta a year now and my wife, children and I hardly saw one another.

It had gotten to the point where I went and saw a lawyer to file for divorce. I wasn't sure of my rights regarding visitation, support, etc. so I needed advice. I then had the attorney draw up the paperwork for divorce.

But in the end, I just couldn't go through with it. I was stuck on the thought that my children would think I had married their mother solely to get a green card and now that I had returned to the United States, I was going to divorce her. That wasn't the case at all, and I just couldn't have them believing anything of the sort.

And then, it all changed in a heartbeat. I got a very good job offer in my field from a tech company called Clarifier located in Roosevelt, Florida.

Chapter 15

WHILE IT WAS A GOOD job that paid well, moving from Atlanta to Florida was difficult. I would be moving to a state further away from my children and also where I knew no one. . It would be a lonely existence, particularly after fighting for so long.

The working environment actually only made it harder for me. Don't get me wrong, the work environment was really great and my co-workers very accepting, but they talked a lot about their families, what they were going to do together on the weekends and the like.

That put me under a lot of stress. I still couldn't figure out what I could do to make my own family life happy and fulfilling again.

I just wouldn't relate to my co-workers in any kind of meaningful way as I didn't want to explain to them what the situation was with my own family. So, I isolated myself so I wouldn't have to explain and just concentrated on my work.

That kind of isolation took its toll on me mentally though. The job was a five-month contract and ended around Christmas time. I didn't have any place to go for Christmas. I wasn't going to be with my children. Indeed my relationship with them had ebbed to almost nil.

I became depressed and suffered from nightmares. I had a new consulting contract offered me beginning in January of the New Year but I was in no state to do the job well so I passed.

I knew what I really needed was to figure out a way to break through the block and communicate effectively with my children.

And then it came to me. I could write a book! Not only would it tell to my children my story and what had happened, dispelling any belief they may have had that I had abandoned them or didn't love them. A book could be the vehicle that would allow me to explain to my kids what happened from my point of view so maybe they could better understand that they were the center of my life, the force that together with my faith, kept me going.

Through the book I could also throw light onto the disaster that is the Immigration Service and the heartbreak that people have to endure because of the stupidity of the actions of the Service. Perhaps what I endured could benefit some who were also being detained, help them in developing a strategy that might aid them somewhat through the legal maze that the Immigration Service hides behind.

And finally, I could make people aware of what was going on regarding the immigration policy that exists today. We have all been told that the system is broken but I could show them how broken it really was, the heartache and distress immigrants are put through.

I was actually one of the lucky ones, not only to have been able in the end to return to the United States and to my family, but that I survived the process at all. Many I had come to know who were in similar situations didn't survive, committing suicide in not being able to be with their families ever again. Others remain in the limbo of waiting and hoping that somehow, someway, someday, they will be reunited with their loved ones.

I decided on a three month break to work and get this out of my system. The process of explaining my story proved therapeutic and even cathartic.

This book is the result of that effort and I pray to the Almighty that it explains more fully to my children what I went through, that they were the strength, together with my faith, that kept me going in those dark times. That my love for them never changed, not to this very day.

I also pray that others who may read this might be compelled to look beneath the news stories about immigrants and come to understand how the current immigration system is stacked against them, serving neither the hopeful immigrant nor the American public.

No system of immigration should force families apart, destroying the integrity of the family and causing the heart wrenching pain such separation entails or enduring it in the hopes of returning home.

In the end, its public opinion that will change that system, and I hope that my small voice may might help to influence that opinion for the better!

www.ingramcontent.com/pod-product-compliance
Lightning Source LLC
Chambersburg PA
CBHW070828180526
45168CB00002B/774